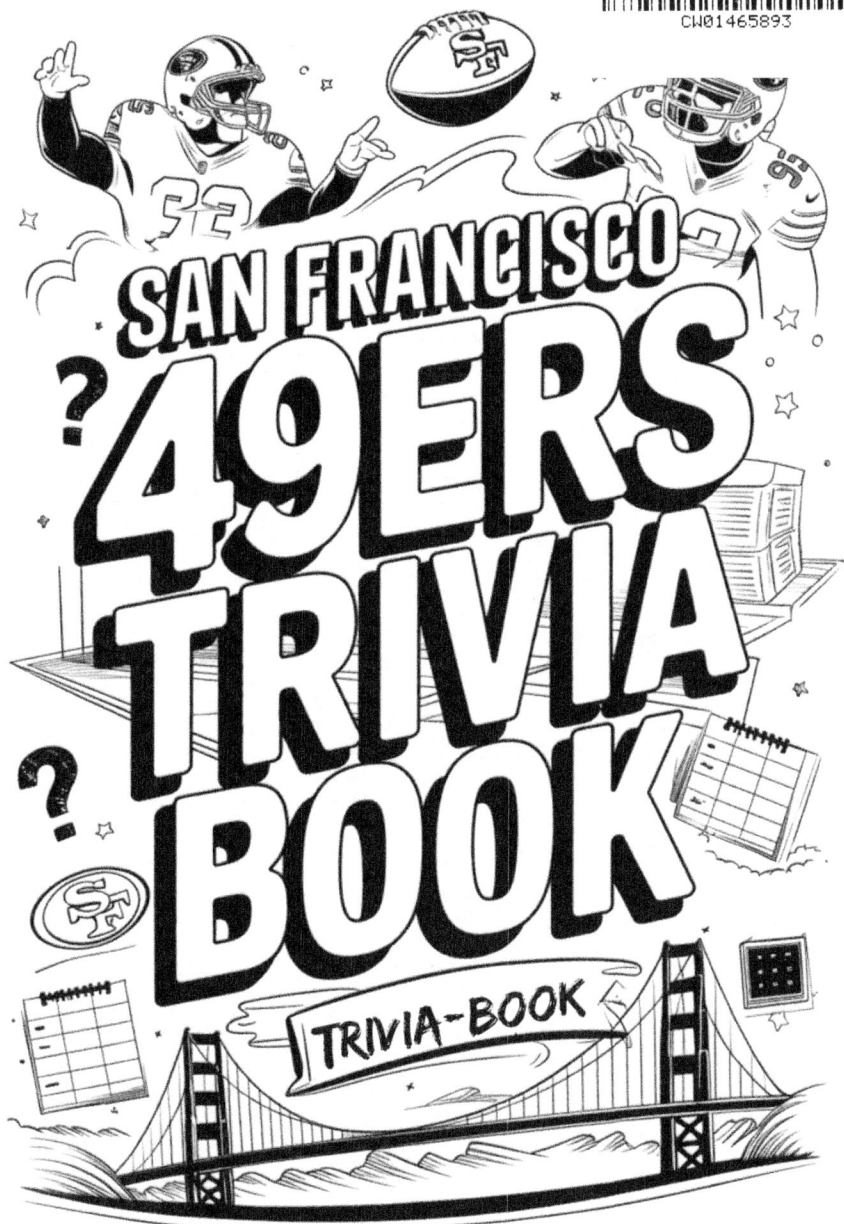

SAN FRANCISCO 49ERS TRIVIA BOOK

TRIVIA-BOOK

TABLE OF CONTENTS

PART I

THE EARLY YEARS AND FORMATION
(1946-1979)

CHAPTER 1:

BORN IN SAN FRANCISCO (1946-1959)

Questions:

1. **What year was the San Francisco 49ers officially founded?**
   A.   1946
   B.   1950
   C.   1935
   D. 1960

---

2. **Which league did the 49ers join at the time of their founding?**
   A. NFL
   B. AAFC
   C. CFL
   D. AFL

---

3. **What was the name of the 49ers' first stadium?**
   A. Kezar Stadium
   B. Levi's Stadium
   C. Candlestick Park
   D. Oakland Coliseum

---

4. **Who was the first owner of the San Francisco 49ers?**
   A. Eddie DeBartolo Sr.
   B. Jed York

C. Tony Morabito
D. George Halas

---

5. **What was the 49ers' first official team color?**
A. Red and White
B. Gold and White
C. Red and Gold
D. Blue and Gold

---

6. **Who was the first head coach of the 49ers?**
A. Buck Shaw
B. George Seifert
C. Bill Walsh
D. Jim Harbaugh

---

7. **What was the result of the 49ers' first-ever game in 1946?**
A. Win
B. Loss
C. Tie
D. Canceled

---

8. **What team did the 49ers face in their inaugural game in 1946?**
A. Chicago Bears
B. Los Angeles Dons
C. Cleveland Browns
D. Pittsburgh Steelers

9. **What unique mascot did the 49ers adopt early?**
   A. A prospector
   B. A bear
   C. A cowboy
   D. A miner's pickaxe

10. **What year did the 49ers join the NFL after the AAFC folded?**
    A. 1950
    B. 1955
    C. 1949
    D. 1960

11. **Who was the team's standout running back in the late 1940s?**
    A. Hugh McElhenny
    B. Joe Perry
    C. Y.A. Tittle
    D. Frank Gore

12. **What was the nickname of the 49ers' famous backfield in the 1950s?**
    A. Fantastic Four
    B. Million Dollar Backfield
    C. Golden Gate Warriors
    D. Red Gold Squad

13. **Which player became the first 49er inducted into the Pro Football Hall of Fame?**
    A. Y.A. Tittle
    B. Joe Perry
    C. Bob St. Clair
    D. Hugh McElhenny

14. **What was the 49ers' record in their inaugural season in 1946?**
    A. 13-1
    B. 9-5
    C. 7-4-1
    D. 2-10

15. **Who was the first quarterback of the San Francisco 49ers?**
    A. Frankie Albert
    B. Steve Young
    C. Joe Montana
    D. Y.A. Tittle

16. **What financial struggles did the team face during its early years?**
    A. Limited fan attendance
    B. Player salary disputes
    C. Owner health crisis
    D. Stadium maintenance issues

17. **What historical event influenced the team's naming?**
    A. California Gold Rush
    B. Opening of the Golden Gate Bridge
    C. Statehood of California
    D. San Francisco Earthquake

18. **What was the team's first AAFC win?**
    A. 4 games
    B. 6 games
    C. 10 games
    D. 8 games

19. **What rival team dominated the AAFC during the 49ers' early years?**
    A. Los Angeles Rams
    B. Cleveland Browns
    C. New York Giants
    D. Green Bay Packers

20. **What innovation did the 49ers introduce in their early games?**
    A. Wide receiver screen
    B. Shotgun formation
    C. First-ever goal post camera
    D. Two-tight-end set

Answers:

1. **Answer:** A. 1946
   Explanation: The San Francisco 49ers were officially

founded in 1946 as a member of the All-America Football Conference (AAFC).

---

2. **Answer:** B. AAFC
   Explanation: The 49ers started in the AAFC, a rival league to the NFL, before the two leagues merged in 1950.

---

3. **Answer:** A. Kezar Stadium
   Explanation: Kezar Stadium in San Francisco served as the 49ers' first home.

---

4. **Answer:** C. Tony Morabito
   Explanation: Tony Morabito, a local lumber magnate, was the original owner and founder of the 49ers.

---

5. **Answer:** C. Red and Gold
   Explanation: The team adopted red and gold to symbolize the California Gold Rush and the state's heritage.

---

6. **Answer:** A. Buck Shaw
   Explanation: Buck Shaw was the team's first head coach and led the 49ers during their AAFC years.

---

7. **Answer:** B. Loss
   Explanation: The 49ers lost their inaugural game in 1946 against the Los Angeles Dons.

---

8. **Answer:** B. Los Angeles Dons
   Explanation: The Los Angeles Dons were their opponents in game one.

---

9. **Answer:** A. A prospector
   Explanation: The mascot represented a prospector, tying to the team's name and the Gold Rush.

---

10. **Answer:** A. 1950
    Explanation: The 49ers joined the NFL in 1950 after the AAFC folded.

---

11. **Answer:** B. Joe Perry
    Explanation: Joe Perry, nicknamed "The Jet," was the team's standout running back in the late 1940s and 1950s.

---

12. **Answer:** B. Million Dollar Backfield
    Explanation: The 49ers' backfield of the 1950s was famously known as the "Million Dollar Backfield."

---

13. **Answer:** B. Joe Perry
    Explanation: Joe Perry became the first 49er inducted into the Pro Football Hall of Fame in 1969.

---

14. **Answer:** C. 7-4-1
    Explanation: The 49ers finished their inaugural AAFC season with a 7-4-1 record.

---

15. **Answer:** A. Frankie Albert
    Explanation: Frankie Albert was the first quarterback and also played a key role in the team's early success.

---

16. **Answer:** C. Owner health crisis
    Explanation: Tony Morabito suffered a heart attack, creating financial uncertainty for the team.

---

17. **Answer:** A. California Gold Rush
    Explanation: The name "49ers" references the miners who came to California during the 1849 Gold Rush.

---

18. **Answer:** D. 8 games
    Explanation: The 49ers' first significant winning streak in the AAFC was an 8-game run.

---

19. **Answer:** B. Cleveland Browns
    Explanation: The Cleveland Browns were the dominant team in the AAFC, often beating the 49ers.

---

20. **Answer:** B. Shotgun formation
    Explanation: The 49ers were among the early adopters of the shotgun formation, revolutionizing football strategies.

CHAPTER 2

The Glory of the "Million Dollar Backfield" (1950s)

Questions:

1. **What nickname was given to the 49ers' backfield in the 1950s?**
   A. Fantastic Four
   B. Million Dollar Backfield
   C. Golden Gate Warriors
   D. Red Gold Squad

---

2. **Who were the four Hall of Famers in the "Million Dollar Backfield"?**
   A. Joe Perry, Y.A. Tittle, Hugh McElhenny, and John Brodie
   B. Y.A. Tittle, Joe Perry, Hugh McElhenny, and John Henry Johnson
   C. Joe Perry, Steve Young, Hugh McElhenny, and Dwight Clark
   D. Y.A. Tittle, Roger Craig, Joe Perry, and Frank Gore

---

3. **What position did Joe Perry play in the "Million Dollar Backfield"?**
   A. Quarterback
   B. Halfback
   C. Fullback
   D. Wide Receiver

---

4. **Which team defeated the 49ers in the 1957 NFL playoffs?**
   A. Cleveland Browns
   B. Detroit Lions
   C. Green Bay Packers
   D. New York Giants

---

5. **What was the final score of the 1957 playoff game against the Detroit Lions?**
   A. 24-21
   B. 31-27
   C. 28-24
   D. 27-21

---

6. **What made the "Million Dollar Backfield" unique in NFL history?**
   A. All members were later inducted into the Pro Football Hall of Fame
   B. They scored the most rushing touchdowns in a single season
   C. They had the highest salaries in the league
   D. They were undefeated in 1957

---

7. **What was the 49ers' record during the 1957 regular season?**
   A. 7-5
   B. 8-4
   C. 9-3
   D. 6-6

---

8. **Which player from the "Million Dollar Backfield" was known as "The Jet"?**
   A. Hugh McElhenny
   B. Joe Perry
   C. Y.A. Tittle
   D. John Henry Johnson

---

9. **What year did the 49ers' "Million Dollar Backfield" peak?**
   A. 1955
   B. 1957
   C. 1952
   D. 1954

---

10. **Which rival team did the 49ers face most often during the 1950s?**
    A. Los Angeles Rams
    B. Detroit Lions
    C. Cleveland Browns
    D. Green Bay Packers

---

11. **What was Y.A. Title's position in the "Million Dollar Backfield"?**
    A. Running Back
    B. Quarterback
    C. Wide Receiver
    D. Tight End

---

12. **Which player in the "Million Dollar Backfield" was known for his versatility and ability to make big plays?**
A. Joe Perry
B. Y.A. Tittle
C. Hugh McElhenny
D. John Henry Johnson

13. **How many Pro Bowls did Hugh McElhenny make during the 1950s?**
A. 4
B. 5
C. 6
D. 7

14. **Which player was the first African American to join the 49ers' "Million Dollar Backfield"?**
A. Joe Perry
B. John Henry Johnson
C. Jim Brown
D. Kenny Washington

15. **What year did the 49ers first meet the Detroit Lions in the playoffs?**
A. 1955
B. 1957
C. 1953
D. 1959

16. **Which team had the most success against the 49ers' "Million Dollar Backfield"?**
    A. Cleveland Browns
    B. Green Bay Packers
    C. Detroit Lions
    D. Los Angeles Rams

17. **How many points did the 49ers lead at halftime in the 1957 playoff game against the Lions?**
    A. 10
    B. 20
    C. 24
    D. 27

18. **Which player was known for his speed and elusiveness in the "Million Dollar Backfield"?**
    A. Hugh McElhenny
    B. Y.A. Tittle
    C. Joe Perry
    D. John Henry Johnson

19. **What was the 49ers' biggest strength during the "Million Dollar Backfield" era?**
    A. Their rushing offense
    B. Their passing defense
    C. Their special teams
    D. Their coaching

20. **What lasting impact did the "Million Dollar Backfield" have on the 49ers' franchise culture?**
    A. Established a tradition of offensive innovation
    B. Created the first NFL fan club
    C. Set a record for defensive touchdowns
    D. Revolutionized special teams play

Answers:

1. **Answer:** B. Million Dollar Backfield
   Explanation: The nickname "Million Dollar Backfield" was given to the 49ers' Hall of Fame players during the 1950s due to their exceptional talent.

2. **Answer:** B. Y.A. Tittle, Joe Perry, Hugh McElhenny, and John Henry Johnson
   Explanation: These four players made up the 49ers' "Million Dollar Backfield," and all were later inducted into the Hall of Fame.

3. **Answer:** C. Fullback
   Explanation: Joe Perry played fullback and was one of the best players in franchise history.

4. **Answer:** B. Detroit Lions
   Explanation: The Detroit Lions defeated the 49ers in the 1957 playoffs in a heartbreaking comeback.

5. **Answer:** D. 27-21
   Explanation: The Lions came back from a 20-point deficit to win 27-21, ending the 49ers' playoff hopes.

6. **Answer:** A. All members were later inducted into the Pro Football Hall of Fame

Explanation: The "Million Dollar Backfield" remains unique in NFL history for having all its members inducted into the Hall of Fame.

---

7. **Answer:** B. 8-4
   Explanation: The 49ers finished the 1957 regular season with an 8-4 record, earning a playoff spot.

---

8. **Answer:** B. Joe Perry
   Explanation: Joe Perry was nicknamed "The Jet" for his incredible speed on the field.

---

9. **Answer:** B. 1957
   Explanation: The 49ers' "Million Dollar Backfield" reached its peak in 1957 with a strong regular season performance.

---

10. **Answer:** A. Los Angeles Rams
    Explanation: The Los Angeles Rams were the 49ers' primary rivals throughout the 1950s, leading to heated matchups.

---

11. **Answer:** B. Quarterback
    Explanation: Y.A. Title was the quarterback of the "Million Dollar Backfield," known for his leadership and passing ability.

---

12. **Answer:** C. Hugh McElhenny
    Explanation: McElhenny was renowned for his agility and ability to make game-changing plays.

---

13. **Answer:** C. 6
    Explanation: Hugh McElhenny was selected to six Pro Bowls during his illustrious career.

---

14. **Answer:** A. Joe Perry
    Explanation: Joe Perry was one of the first African American stars in professional football and a key player in the backfield.

---

15. **Answer:** B. 1957
    Explanation: The 49ers first faced the Detroit Lions in the playoffs during the 1957 season.

---

16. **Answer:** C. Detroit Lions
    Explanation: The Lions often succeeded against the 49ers, including their comeback win in the 1957 playoffs.

---

17. **Answer:** C. 24
    Explanation: The 49ers led by 24 points at halftime during the 1957 playoff game, only to lose the lead.

---

18. **Answer:** A. Hugh McElhenny
    Explanation: McElhenny was known for his speed and elusiveness, earning him a spot in the Hall of Fame.

---

19. **Answer:** A. Their rushing offense
    Explanation: The "Million Dollar Backfield" was known for its dominance in rushing the ball.

---

20. **Answer:** A. Established a tradition of offensive innovation
    Explanation: The success of the "Million Dollar Backfield" set a precedent for offensive creativity in the 49ers' franchise.

Chapter 3

Finding an Identity (1960-1979)

Questions:

1. **Who was hired as San Francisco 49ers head coach in 1968?**
   A. Bill Walsh
   B. Dick Nolan
   C. Buck Shaw
   D. George Seifert

2. **Under Dick Nolan, what defensive strategy became the 49ers' hallmark in the 1970s?**
   A. West Coast Offense
   B. Flex Defense
   C. Zone Blitz
   D. 3-4 Defense

3. **What year did the 49ers make their first playoff appearance?**
   A. 1969
   B. 1970
   C. 1972
   D. 1975

4. **What was the result of the 49ers' first playoff game in 1970?**
   A. Victory against the Dallas Cowboys

B. Loss to the Dallas Cowboys
C. Victory against the Green Bay Packers
D. Loss to the Minnesota Vikings

---

5. **Who was the 49ers' starting quarterback during their 1970 playoff run?**
   A. Joe Montana
   B. Steve Spurrier
   C. John Brodie
   D. Y.A. Tittle

---

6. **Which player was known as the 49ers' star wide receiver during the 1970s?**
   A. Dwight Clark
   B. Gene Washington
   C. Jerry Rice
   D. Ken Willard

---

7. **What nickname was given to the 49ers' defense during Dick Nolan's era?**
   A. Gold Rush Defense
   B. Red Wall Defense
   C. The Doomsday Defense
   D. Bruising Rush

---

8. **Which team eliminated the 49ers from the playoffs in both 1970 and 1971?**
   A. Green Bay Packers
   B. Dallas Cowboys

C. Minnesota Vikings
D. Chicago Bears

---

9. **What year did the 49ers win their first NFC West Division title?**
   A. 1968
   B. 1969
   C. 1970
   D. 1972

---

10. **What major challenge did the 49ers face in the mid-1970s?**
   A. Key player retirements
   B. Financial instability
   C. Lack of a consistent quarterback
   D. Relocation to a new city

---

11. **Who was the 49ers' leading rusher in the early 1970s?**
   A. Roger Craig
   B. Hugh McElhenny
   C. Ken Willard
   D. Delvin Williams

---

12. **What was the name of the 49ers' home stadium during this era?**
   A. Levi's Stadium
   B. Kezar Stadium

C. Candlestick Park
D. Spartan Stadium

13. **Which 49ers player was named 1970 NFL MVP?**
    A. Gene Washington
    B. John Brodie
    C. Y.A. Tittle
    D. Joe Montana

14. **How many consecutive playoff appearances did the 49ers achieve under Dick Nolan?**
    A. 1
    B. 2
    C. 3
    D. 4

15. **What team did the 49ers defeat in their first-ever playoff victory?**
    A. Green Bay Packers
    B. Dallas Cowboys
    C. Minnesota Vikings
    D. New York Giants

16. **What was one of the 49ers' biggest weaknesses during the late 1970s?**
    A. Poor offensive line
    B. Inconsistent quarterback play
    C. Weak secondary defense
    D. Inexperienced coaching staff

17. **What notable player joined the 49ers in the 1970s and later became a Hall of Famer?**
    A. Roger Craig
    B. Joe Montana
    C. Fred Dean
    D. O.J. Simpson

18. **Which team became the 49ers' main rival during the 1970s?**
    A. Los Angeles Rams
    B. Dallas Cowboys
    C. Green Bay Packers
    D. Pittsburgh Steelers

19. **What was the 49ers' record in their 1970 division-winning season?**
    A. 10-3-1
    B. 11-3
    C. 9-5
    D. 12-2

20. **How did Dick Nolan's leadership affect 49ers franchise culture?**
    A. Established a strong defensive identity
    B. Revolutionized the passing game
    C. Focused on special teams innovation
    D. Improved financial stability

Answers:

1. **Answer:** B. Dick Nolan
   Explanation: Dick Nolan was hired as head coach in 1968 and led the 49ers to multiple playoff appearances.

2. **Answer:** B. Flex Defense
   Explanation: Nolan introduced the "Flex Defense," which became a key part of the 49ers' success in the 1970s.

3. **Answer:** B. 1970
   Explanation: The 49ers made their first playoff appearance in 1970 after winning the NFC West Division.

4. **Answer:** B. Loss to the Dallas Cowboys
   Explanation: The 49ers lost to the Dallas Cowboys in their first playoff game in 1970.

5. **Answer:** C. John Brodie
   Explanation: John Brodie was the 49ers' quarterback during the 1970 playoff run and won the NFL MVP that year.

6. **Answer:** B. Gene Washington
   Explanation: Gene Washington was the team's leading receiver and a two-time Pro Bowl selection.

---

7. **Answer:** A. Gold Rush Defense
   Explanation: The "Gold Rush Defense" was the nickname for the 49ers' defense under Nolan's leadership.

---

8. **Answer:** B. Dallas Cowboys
   Explanation: The Cowboys eliminated the 49ers from the playoffs in both 1970 and 1971.

---

9. **Answer:** C. 1970
   Explanation: The 49ers won the NFC West Division title for the first time in 1970.

---

10. **Answer:** A. Key player retirements
    Explanation: The 49ers faced significant challenges in the mid-1970s as key players retired or left the team.

---

11. **Answer:** C. Ken Willard
    Explanation: Ken Willard was the team's leading rusher in the early 1970s and a key offensive contributor.

---

12. **Answer:** C. Candlestick Park
    Explanation: The 49ers moved to Candlestick Park in 1971, which became their home for decades.

---

13. **Answer:** B. John Brodie
    Explanation: John Brodie won the 1970 NFL MVP award for his outstanding performance.

---

14. **Answer:** C. 3
    Explanation: The 49ers made three consecutive playoff appearances under Dick Nolan from 1970 to 1972.

---

15. **Answer:** A. Green Bay Packers
    Explanation: The 49ers defeated the Packers in their first-ever playoff victory in 1970.

---

16. **Answer:** B. Inconsistent quarterback play
    Explanation: The team struggled with inconsistent quarterback performances in the late 1970s.

---

17. **Answer:** D. O.J. Simpson
    Explanation: O.J. Simpson joined the 49ers in the late 1970s and became a Hall of Famer.

---

18. **Answer:** A. Los Angeles Rams
    Explanation: The Rams and 49ers developed a heated

rivalry during the 1970s, particularly in NFC West matchups.

---

19. **Answer:** A. 10-3-1
    Explanation: The 49ers finished the 1970 season with a 10-3-1 record, securing the NFC West title.

---

20. **Answer:** A. Established a strong defensive identity
    Explanation: Nolan's leadership emphasized defense, laying the groundwork for the 49ers' future success.

PART II:

THE GOLDEN ERA AND DYNASTY YEARS (1980-1999)

Chapter 4: The Joe Montana Era Begins (1980-1984)

Questions:

1. **Who became the head coach of the San Francisco 49ers in 1979, ushering in a new era for the team?**
   A. George Seifert
   B. Dick Nolan
   C. Bill Walsh
   D. Mike Holmgren

2. **What offensive strategy did Bill Walsh introduce to the 49ers?**
   A. Air Raid Offense
   B. West Coast Offense
   C. Spread Offense
   D. Run and Shoot

3. **What year was Joe Montana drafted by the San Francisco 49ers?**
   A. 1977
   B. 1979
   C. 1980
   D. 1981

4. **What NFL Draft round was Joe Montana selected in?**
   A. First round
   B. Second round

C. Third round
D. Fourth round

---

5. **What was the nickname of the 49ers' dramatic playoff win against the Dallas Cowboys in the 1981 NFC Championship Game?**
   A. The Drive
   B. The Miracle
   C. The Catch
   D. The Leap

---

6. **Who caught the game-winning touchdown in "The Catch"?**
   A. Jerry Rice
   B. Dwight Clark
   C. John Taylor
   D. Roger Craig

---

7. **What year did the 49ers win their first Super Bowl?**
   A. 1980
   B. 1981
   C. 1983
   D. 1984

---

8. **Which team did the 49ers defeat in their first Super Bowl victory?**
   A. Miami Dolphins
   B. Cincinnati Bengals

C. Pittsburgh Steelers
D. Dallas Cowboys

---

9. **What was the final score of Super Bowl XVI, the 49ers' first championship game?**
    A. 26-21
    B. 20-17
    C. 27-24
    D. 28-10

---

10. **Who was named MVP of Super Bowl XVI?**
    A. Roger Craig
    B. Joe Montana
    C. Dwight Clark
    D. Ronnie Lott

---

11. **What defensive star was a key player for the 49ers during their 1981 Super Bowl season?**
    A. Charles Haley
    B. Fred Dean
    C. Ronnie Lott
    D. Patrick Willis

---

12. **Which 49ers player became known for his versatility and ability to score rushing and receiving touchdowns in the early 1980s?**
    A. Roger Craig
    B. Tom Rathman

C. Wendell Tyler
D. Dwight Clark

---

13. **What team eliminated the 49ers from the playoffs in the 1983 season?**
A. Dallas Cowboys
B. Miami Dolphins
C. Washington Redskins
D. New York Giants

---

14. **What record did Joe Montana set during the 1981 season?**
A. Most passing touchdowns in a season
B. Most fourth-quarter comebacks
C. Highest passer rating in a season
D. Most passing yards in a season

---

15. **How did the West Coast Offense revolutionize football strategy?**
A. Focused on deep throws and vertical passing
B. Emphasized short, accurate passes and yards after catch
C. Relied heavily on running backs for rushing yards
D. Introduced the no-huddle offense

---

16. **What is the lasting legacy of "The Catch"?**
A. Cemented the Cowboys' dominance over the 49ers
B. Marked the beginning of the 49ers dynasty

C. Was the highest-scoring game in NFL history

D. Led to rule changes in the NFL

17. **Which player became the 49ers' defensive leader and was known for his hard-hitting style?**
    A. Ronnie Lott
    B. Fred Dean
    C. Patrick Willis
    D. Charles Haley

18. **How many touchdowns did Joe Montana score in Super Bowl XVI?**
    A. 1
    B. 2
    C. 3
    D. 4

19. **Who was the 49ers' leading receiver during their 1981 Super Bowl season?**
    A. Dwight Clark
    B. Jerry Rice
    C. John Taylor
    D. Freddie Solomon

20. **What was one of the biggest challenges the 49ers faced during the early Joe Montana era?**
    A. Weak offensive line
    B. Inexperienced coaching staff

C. Poor defensive depth
D. Overcoming a history of losing seasons

Answers:

1. **Answer:** C. Bill Walsh
   Explanation: Bill Walsh became the head coach in 1979 and transformed the franchise with his innovative strategies.

2. **Answer:** B. West Coast Offense
   Explanation: The West Coast Offense focused on short, precise passing and was a hallmark of Walsh's coaching style.

3. **Answer:** B. 1979
   Explanation: Joe Montana was drafted in 1979 from Notre Dame.

4. **Answer:** C. Third round
   Explanation: Montana was selected in the third round of the 1979 NFL Draft, a steal for the 49ers.

5. **Answer:** C. The Catch
   Explanation: "The Catch" refers to Dwight Clark's iconic game-winning touchdown in the 1981 NFC Championship Game.

6. **Answer:** B. Dwight Clark
    Explanation: Dwight Clark made the legendary leaping grab from a pass by Joe Montana.

---

7. **Answer:** B. 1981
    Explanation: The 49ers won their first Super Bowl in the 1981 season.

---

8. **Answer:** B. Cincinnati Bengals
    Explanation: The 49ers defeated the Bengals 26-21 in Super Bowl XVI.

---

9. **Answer:** A. 26-21
    Explanation: The 49ers edged out the Bengals in a tightly contested Super Bowl.

---

10. **Answer:** B. Joe Montana
    Explanation: Montana was named MVP for his exceptional performance in Super Bowl XVI.

---

11. **Answer:** C. Ronnie Lott
    Explanation: Lott was a dominant defender during the 1981 season.

---

12. **Answer:** A. Roger Craig
Explanation: Craig's ability to score both rushing and receiving touchdowns made him a standout.

---

13. **Answer:** C. Washington Redskins
Explanation: The Redskins eliminated the 49ers in the 1983 NFC Championship Game.

---

14. **Answer:** B. Most fourth-quarter comebacks
Explanation: Montana became known for his ability to lead game-winning drives late in games.

---

15. **Answer:** B. Emphasized short, accurate passes and yards after catch
Explanation: The West Coast Offense revolutionized the way offenses attacked defenses.

---

16. **Answer:** B. Marked the beginning of the 49ers dynasty
Explanation: "The Catch" symbolized a turning point, leading to years of success for the team.

---

17. **Answer:** A. Ronnie Lott
Explanation: Lott was a fearsome tackler and the leader of the defense.

---

18. **Answer:** A. 1
    Explanation: Montana accounted for one touchdown in Super Bowl XVI but managed the game effectively.

---

19. **Answer:** A. Dwight Clark
    Explanation: Clark led the team in receiving yards and was a key player in the 1981 season.

---

20. **Answer:** D. Overcoming a history of losing seasons
    Explanation: The 49ers had struggled for years before Walsh and Montana's arrival turned the team around.

Chapter 5

A Dynasty Is Born (1985-1990)

Questions:

1. **What year did Jerry Rice join the San Francisco 49ers?**
   A. 1983
   B. 1984
   C. 1985
   D. 1986

---

2. **Which college did Jerry Rice play for before joining the NFL?**
   A. Notre Dame
   B. Mississippi Valley State
   C. USC
   D. Alabama

---

3. **What record did Jerry Rice set in the 1987 NFL season?**
   A. Most receiving yards in a season
   B. Most touchdowns in a season
   C. Most receptions in a season
   D. Most games with 100+ receiving yards

---

4. **Who was the 49ers head coach during their back-to-back Super Bowl wins in 1988 and 1989?**
   A. Bill Walsh

B. George Seifert
C. Mike Shanahan
D. Steve Mariucci

---

5. **What was the 49ers' record during the 1989 regular season?**
   A. 14-2
   B. 12-4
   C. 13-3
   D. 15-1

---

6. **Which team did the 49ers defeat in Super Bowl XXIII?**
   A. Miami Dolphins
   B. Cincinnati Bengals
   C. Dallas Cowboys
   D. Denver Broncos

---

7. **What was the final score of Super Bowl XXIII?**
   A. 20-16
   B. 28-10
   C. 27-24
   D. 31-21

---

8. **What iconic drive led to the 49ers' Super Bowl XXIII victory?**
   A. "The Catch II"
   B. "The Drive"

C. "The Montana Miracle"
D. "The Final Drive"

9. **Which player caught the game-winning touchdown in Super Bowl XXIII?**
   A. Jerry Rice
   B. John Taylor
   C. Roger Craig
   D. Brent Jones

10. **Who was named Super Bowl MVP in Super Bowl XXIII?**
    A. Joe Montana
    B. Jerry Rice
    C. John Taylor
    D. Ronnie Lott

11. **Which team did the 49ers defeat in Super Bowl XXIV?**
    A. Cincinnati Bengals
    B. Miami Dolphins
    C. Denver Broncos
    D. Dallas Cowboys

12. **What was the score of the 49ers' dominant victory in Super Bowl XXIV?**
    A. 55-10
    B. 48-14

C. 42-17
D. 31-10

---

13. **Who was named MVP of Super Bowl XXIV?**
    A. Joe Montana
    B. Jerry Rice
    C. Roger Craig
    D. John Taylor

---

14. **What rivalry became particularly intense during the late 1980s?**
    A. 49ers vs. Dallas Cowboys
    B. 49ers vs. New York Giants
    C. 49ers vs. Green Bay Packers
    D. 49ers vs. Los Angeles Rams

---

15. **Which defensive player became a cornerstone for the 49ers during this era?**
    A. Ronnie Lott
    B. Fred Dean
    C. Charles Haley
    D. Patrick Willis

---

16. **What team eliminated the 49ers from the playoffs in the 1986 and 1990 seasons?**
    A. New York Giants
    B. Dallas Cowboys
    C. Washington Redskins
    D. Green Bay Packers

17. **What record did Joe Montana set during the 1989 season?**
    A. Highest single-season passer rating
    B. Most touchdown passes in a season
    C. Longest touchdown pass in history
    D. Most completions in a season

18. **What innovation was credited with the 49ers' offensive success during this period?**
    A. Zone running scheme
    B. Enhanced West Coast Offense
    C. Spread Offense
    D. No-huddle offense

19. **Who was the 49ers' offensive coordinator during their back-to-back Super Bowl wins?**
    A. Mike Shanahan
    B. Mike Holmgren
    C. Steve Mariucci
    D. Norv Turner

20. **How many total Super Bowls did the 49ers win during the Joe Montana and Jerry Rice era?**
    A. 2
    B. 3
    C. 4
    D. 5

Answers:

1. **Answer:** C. 1985
    Explanation: Jerry Rice was drafted by the 49ers in the 1985 NFL Draft.

2. **Answer:** B. Mississippi Valley State
    Explanation: Rice played at a small school but dominated with his incredible skill.

3. **Answer:** B. Most touchdowns in a season
    Explanation: Rice scored 22 touchdowns in 1987 despite a shortened season.

4. **Answer:** B. George Seifert
    Explanation: Seifert succeeded Bill Walsh and coached the team to consecutive Super Bowl wins.

5. **Answer:** A. 14-2
    Explanation: The 49ers had a dominant 1989 season with a 14-2 record.

6. **Answer:** B. Cincinnati Bengals
    Explanation: The 49ers defeated the Bengals 20-16 in Super Bowl XXIII.

7. **Answer:** A. 20-16
   Explanation: The game was decided by a late-game drive led by Montana.

---

8. **Answer:** D. "The Final Drive"
   Explanation: Montana orchestrated a 92-yard drive, capped by the game-winning touchdown.

---

9. **Answer:** B. John Taylor
   Explanation: Taylor caught the touchdown that secured the 49ers victory.

---

10. **Answer:** B. Jerry Rice
    Explanation: Rice was named MVP for his record-breaking performance in Super Bowl XXIII.

---

11. **Answer:** C. Denver Broncos
    Explanation: The 49ers routed the Broncos 55-10 in Super Bowl XXIV.

---

12. **Answer:** A. 55-10
    Explanation: The 49ers delivered the most lopsided victory in Super Bowl history.

---

13. **Answer:** A. Joe Montana
    Explanation: Montana was named MVP for his near-perfect performance in Super Bowl XXIV.

---

14. **Answer:** B. 49ers vs. New York Giants
    Explanation: The Giants became a key rival, defeating the 49ers in critical playoff games.

---

15. **Answer:** C. Charles Haley
    Explanation: Haley was a dominant pass rusher and a key part of the defense.

---

16. **Answer:** A. New York Giants
    Explanation: The Giants eliminated the 49ers from the playoffs in 1986 and 1990.

---

17. **Answer:** A. Highest single-season passer rating
    Explanation: Montana achieved a passer rating of 112.4 in the 1989 season, a record at the time.

---

18. **Answer:** B. Enhanced West Coast Offense
    Explanation: Bill Walsh's system was refined and optimized for Montana and Rice.

---

19. **Answer:** A. Mike Shanahan
    Explanation: Shanahan served as the offensive coordinator, playing a key role in their success.

---

20. **Answer:** C. 4
    Explanation: The 49ers won four Super Bowls during the Montana and Rice era: 1981, 1984, 1988, and 1989.

Chapter 6

The Steve Young Years (1991-1999)

Questions:

1. **What year did Steve Young officially become the starting quarterback for the 49ers?**
   A. 1990
   B. 1991
   C. 1992
   D. 1993

2. **Which team did the 49ers trade Joe Montana in 1993?**
   A. Kansas City Chiefs
   B. Denver Broncos
   C. Miami Dolphins
   D. Green Bay Packers

3. **What was Steve Young's playing style best known for?**
   A. Pocket passing
   B. Mobile quarterbacking and scrambling ability
   C. Deep passing accuracy
   D. Defensive play-calling

4. **Which Hall of Fame receiver was Steve Young's primary target during the 1990s?**
   A. Terrell Owens

B. Dwight Clark
C. John Taylor
D. Jerry Rice

---

5. **What year did the 49ers win the Super Bowl with Steve Young as their starting quarterback?**
   A. 1993
   B. 1994
   C. 1995
   D. 1996

---

6. **Which team did the 49ers defeat in Super Bowl XXIX?**
   A. San Diego Chargers
   B. Miami Dolphins
   C. Dallas Cowboys
   D. Buffalo Bills

---

7. **What was Super Bowl XXIX's score?**
   A. 49-26
   B. 35-24
   C. 28-10
   D. 42-17

---

8. **How many touchdown passes did Steve Young throw in Super Bowl XXIX?**
   A. 4
   B. 5

C. 6
D. 7

---

9. **Who was named MVP of Super Bowl XXIX?**
   A. Jerry Rice
   B. Steve Young
   C. Ricky Watters
   D. Brent Jones

---

10. **Which team was the 49ers' biggest rival during the mid-1990s?**
    A. Green Bay Packers
    B. Dallas Cowboys
    C. New York Giants
    D. Seattle Seahawks

---

11. **What challenge did the 49ers face in the salary cap era of the late 1990s?**
    A. Difficulty retaining star players
    B. Lack of draft picks
    C. Injuries to key players
    D. Declining fan support

---

12. **Which player emerged as the 49ers' new offensive weapon in the late 1990s?**
    A. Frank Gore
    B. Terrell Owens
    C. Jeff Garcia
    D. Garrison Hearst

13. **Which defensive star was a consistent force for the 49ers during the Steve Young years?**
    A. Charles Haley
    B. Ronnie Lott
    C. Bryant Young
    D. Fred Dean

14. **What injury eventually ended Steve Young's career?**
    A. Knee injury
    B. Concussion
    C. Shoulder injury
    D. Torn Achilles

15. **In which year did the 49ers fail to make the playoffs for the first time in the 1990s?**
    A. 1997
    B. 1998
    C. 1999
    D. 1995

16. **How many NFC Championship Games did the 49ers play in the 1990s?**
    A. 2
    B. 3
    C. 4
    D. 5

17. **What was Steve Young's passer rating in the 1994 season, which led the league?**
    A. 112.8
    B. 107.6
    C. 110.5
    D. 104.3

18. **Who succeeded Steve Young as the 49ers' starting quarterback after his retirement?**
    A. Alex Smith
    B. Jeff Garcia
    C. Colin Kaepernick
    D. Tim Rattay

19. **Which team eliminated the 49ers from the playoffs in 1998?**
    A. Dallas Cowboys
    B. Green Bay Packers
    C. Atlanta Falcons
    D. Minnesota Vikings

20. **What legacy did the 49ers leave in the late 1990s?**
    A. Decline of a dynasty but a foundation for future success
    B. Dominance as the league's most consistent playoff team
    C. Rebuilding phase without star players
    D. New rivalries formed

Answers:

1. **Answer:** B. 1991
   Explanation: Steve Young became the quarterback in 1991 after Joe Montana's injury.

2. **Answer:** A. Kansas City Chiefs
   Explanation: Montana was traded to the Chiefs in 1993, marking the end of an era in San Francisco.

3. **Answer:** B. Mobile quarterbacking and scrambling ability
   Explanation: Young was known for his mobility and ability to extend plays with his legs.

4. **Answer:** D. Jerry Rice
   Explanation: Rice remained the primary receiver during Young's tenure, maintaining his Hall of Fame-level production.

5. **Answer:** B. 1994
   Explanation: The 49ers won Super Bowl XXIX during the 1994 season with Steve Young as the quarterback.

6. **Answer:** A. San Diego Chargers
   Explanation: The 49ers defeated the Chargers 49-26 in Super Bowl XXIX.

7. **Answer:** A. 49-26
   Explanation: The 49ers dominated the Chargers in one of the most lopsided Super Bowls in history.

8. **Answer:** C. 6
   Explanation: Young threw a record six touchdown passes in Super Bowl XXIX.

9. **Answer:** B. Steve Young
   Explanation: Young was named MVP for his historic performance in Super Bowl XXIX.

10. **Answer:** B. Dallas Cowboys
    Explanation: The Cowboys were a major rival, clashing with the 49ers multiple times in the playoffs.

11. **Answer:** A. Difficulty retaining star players
    Explanation: The salary cap limited the 49ers' ability to keep their roster intact in the late 1990s.

12. **Answer:** B. Terrell Owens
    Explanation: Owens became a key offensive weapon during the late 1990s.

13. **Answer:** C. Bryant Young
    Explanation: Bryant Young was a standout defensive lineman and leader for the team.

---

14. **Answer:** B. Concussion
    Explanation: Young's career ended due to multiple concussions, with the final one occurring in 1999.

---

15. **Answer:** C. 1999
    Explanation: The 49ers missed the playoffs in 1999, marking the end of their dominance.

---

16. **Answer:** D. 5
    Explanation: The 49ers played in five NFC Championship Games during the 1990s.

---

17. **Answer:** A. 112.8
    Explanation: Young's passer rating of 112.8 in 1994 led the league and was among the highest in NFL history at the time.

---

18. **Answer:** B. Jeff Garcia
    Explanation: Garcia succeeded Young as the starting quarterback, leading the team into the early 2000s.

---

19. **Answer:** C. Atlanta Falcons
    Explanation: The Falcons eliminated the 49ers in the 1998 playoffs.

---

20. **Answer:** A. Decline of a dynasty but a foundation for future success
    Explanation: While the 49ers faced challenges in the late 1990s, their legacy of success endured.

PART III

REBUILDING AND MODERN SUCCESS (2000-PRESENT)

Chapter 7

Struggles and Changes (2000-2010)

Questions:

1. **Who became the head coach of the 49ers in 2000, starting the decade of struggles and changes?**
   A. Steve Mariucci
   B. Dennis Erickson
   C. Steve Mariucci
   D. Mike Nolan

2. **Which quarterback started the most games for the 49ers during the 2000 season?**
   A. Jeff Garcia
   B. Tim Rattay
   C. Alex Smith
   D. Steve Young

3. **What was the 49ers' 2004 season record, one of the worst in franchise history?**
   A. 2-14
   B. 4-12
   C. 6-10
   D. 3-13

4. **Which player emerged as the 49ers' star running back during the mid-2000s?**
   A. Kevan Barlow

B. Frank Gore
C. Garrison Hearst
D. Ricky Watters

---

5. **What year was Frank Gore drafted by the 49ers?**
   A. 2003
   B. 2004
   C. 2005
   D. 2006

---

6. **Who was the 49ers' first overall draft pick in 2005?**
   A. Alex Smith
   B. Aaron Rodgers
   C. Frank Gore
   D. Patrick Willis

---

7. **Which coach began rebuilding the 49ers' defense with young talent in 2005?**
   A. Mike Nolan
   B. Mike Singletary
   C. Dennis Erickson
   D. Jim Harbaugh

---

8. **What nickname was given to the 49ers' developing defense in the late 2000s?**
   A. The Red Wall
   B. The Gold Rush
   C. The New Front
   D. The Brick Squad

9. **What major challenge did the 49ers face during the 2000s coaching carousel?**
   A. Difficulty attracting free agents
   B. Frequent injuries to star players
   C. Lack of consistency in leadership
   D. Declining fan interest

10. **In which year did Frank Gore rush for over 2,000 all-purpose yards?**
    A. 2005
    B. 2006
    C. 2007
    D. 2008

11. **Who replaced Mike Nolan as head coach in 2008?**
    A. Mike Singletary
    B. Jim Harbaugh
    C. Steve Mariucci
    D. Dennis Erickson

12. **Which stadium was home to the 49ers throughout the 2000s?**
    A. Kezar Stadium
    B. Levi's Stadium
    C. Candlestick Park
    D. Oracle Park

13. **Who was the 49ers' leading wide receiver during most of the 2000s?**
    A. Terrell Owens
    B. Anquan Boldin
    C. Brandon Lloyd
    D. Michael Crabtree

14. **What was the 49ers' best season record during the 2000-2010 period?**
    A. 7-9
    B. 8-8
    C. 9-7
    D. 10-6

15. **Which quarterback did the 49ers draft as the first overall pick in 2005?**
    A. Tim Rattay
    B. Alex Smith
    C. Colin Kaepernick
    D. Blaine Gabbert

16. **Which player became the heart of the 49ers' defense in the late 2000s?**
    A. Patrick Willis
    B. NaVorro Bowman
    C. Justin Smith
    D. Ahmad Brooks

17. **What slogan did Mike Singletary use to inspire his team?**
A. "Do your job."
B. "Win with honor."
C. "We want winners."
D. "Brick by brick."

18. **Which team became the 49ers' consistent rival in the NFC West during the 2000s?**
A. Los Angeles Rams
B. Seattle Seahawks
C. Arizona Cardinals
D. St. Louis Rams

19. **What was one major success of the 49ers' rebuilding efforts by the end of the 2000s?**
A. Drafting future stars like Patrick Willis and Joe Staley
B. Reaching the playoffs
C. Winning the NFC West
D. Hiring Jim Harbaugh

20. **What legacy did the 49ers leave after their struggles in the 2000s?**
A. A foundation of young talent and leadership
B. A decline in fan engagement
C. A complete rebuild with a new coaching staff
D. Loss of relevance in the NFC

Answers:

1. **Answer:** C. Steve Mariucci
   Explanation: Steve Mariucci began the decade as head coach, though he was replaced during the struggles.

2. **Answer:** A. Jeff Garcia
   Explanation: Jeff Garcia was the starting quarterback and a bright spot for the team in the early 2000s.

3. **Answer:** A. 2-14
   Explanation: The 49ers had their worst 2004 season, 2-14.

4. **Answer:** B. Frank Gore
   Explanation: Gore emerged as a star running back and became the cornerstone of the 49ers' offense.

5. **Answer:** C. 2005
   Explanation: Frank Gore was drafted in the third round of the 2005 NFL Draft.

6. **Answer:** A. Alex Smith
   Explanation: The 49ers selected Alex Smith as the first overall pick in 2005.

7. **Answer:** A. Mike Nolan
   Explanation: Nolan focused on rebuilding the defense with young players, laying a new foundation.

---

8. **Answer:** B. The Gold Rush
   Explanation: The defense was nicknamed "The Gold Rush" as it began showing promise.

---

9. **Answer:** C. Lack of consistency in leadership
   Explanation: Frequent coaching changes hurt team stability and progress.

---

10. **Answer:** B. 2006
    Explanation: Frank Gore had a breakout year in 2006, rushing for over 2,000 all-purpose yards.

---

11. **Answer:** A. Mike Singletary
    Explanation: Singletary replaced Nolan and became known for his passionate leadership style.

---

12. **Answer:** C. Candlestick Park
    Explanation: The 49ers continued playing at Candlestick Park during the 2000s.

---

13. **Answer:** D. Michael Crabtree
    Explanation: Crabtree was a top receiver for the 49ers in the late 2000s.

---

14. **Answer:** B. 8-8
    Explanation: The 49ers' best record during this decade was 8-8, reflecting their struggles.

---

15. **Answer:** B. Alex Smith
    Explanation: Smith was drafted first overall in 2005 as the 49ers' quarterback of the future.

---

16. **Answer:** A. Patrick Willis
    Explanation: Willis became the 49ers' defensive leader and a perennial Pro Bowler.

---

17. **Answer:** C. "We want winners."
    Explanation: Singletary's motivational slogan became iconic during his tenure.

---

18. **Answer:** B. Seattle Seahawks
    Explanation: The Seahawks became a strong rival in the NFC West during the 2000s.

---

19. **Answer:** A. Drafting future stars like Patrick Willis and Joe Staley

Explanation: The 49ers built a strong foundation by drafting key players for the next era.

---

20. **Answer:** A. A foundation of young talent and leadership
    Explanation: Despite struggles, the team set the stage for future success with a solid core of players.

Chapter 8

The Harbaugh Years (2011-2014)

Questions:

1. **What year did Jim Harbaugh become the head coach of the San Francisco 49ers?**
   A. 2010
   B. 2011
   C. 2012
   D. 2013

---

2. **Which team did the 49ers face in their first playoff game under Jim Harbaugh?**
   A. Green Bay Packers
   B. New Orleans Saints
   C. Seattle Seahawks
   D. Atlanta Falcons

---

3. **What was the nickname of the game Vernon Davis caught the game-winning touchdown against the Saints?**
   A. The Miracle Catch
   B. The Drive
   C. The Catch III
   D. The Vernon Post

---

4. **Who was the 49ers' starting quarterback at the beginning of the 2012 season?**

A. Alex Smith
B. Colin Kaepernick
C. Blaine Gabbert
D. Tim Rattay

5. **What event led to Colin Kaepernick becoming the starting quarterback in 2012?**
A. Alex Smith's injury
B. A coaching decision by Jim Harbaugh
C. Poor team performance
D. A trade involving Alex Smith

6. **What record did Colin Kaepernick set in the 2012 NFC Divisional Round against the Green Bay Packers?**
A. Most rushing yards by a quarterback in a playoff game
B. Most passing touchdowns in a playoff game
C. Longest touchdown run by a quarterback
D. Most combined yards in a playoff game

7. **Which team did the 49ers defeat in the 2012 NFC Championship Game to reach Super Bowl XLVII?**
A. Seattle Seahawks
B. Atlanta Falcons
C. Green Bay Packers
D. New York Giants

8. **Who was the head coach of the Baltimore Ravens during Super Bowl XLVII?**
   A. John Harbaugh
   B. Pete Carroll
   C. Bill Belichick
   D. Andy Reid

9. **What was Super Bowl XLVII's final score?**
   A. 34-31
   B. 31-28
   C. 28-24
   D. 27-20

10. **What was the nickname given to Super Bowl XLVII, where the Harbaugh brothers faced?**
    A. The Brothers Bowl
    B. The Family Bowl
    C. The Harbaugh Bowl
    D. Super Bowl Showdown

11. **Which 49ers player returned a kickoff for a touchdown in Super Bowl XLVII?**
    A. Colin Kaepernick
    B. Michael Crabtree
    C. LaMichael James
    D. Jacoby Jones

12. **What controversial play happened in the final moments of Super Bowl XLVII?**

A. A missed pass interference call

B. A fumble on the goal line

C. A botched snap

D. A roughing the passer penalty

---

13. **What team eliminated the 49ers in the 2013 NFC Championship Game?**
    A. Green Bay Packers
    B. Atlanta Falcons
    C. Seattle Seahawks
    D. New Orleans Saints

---

14. **What was the outcome of the famous "Richard Sherman tip" play in the 2013 NFC Championship Game?**
    A. An interception that sealed the Seahawks' victory
    B. A touchdown by the 49ers
    C. A pass interference penalty on the Seahawks
    D. A first down for the 49ers

---

15. **What defensive player became a cornerstone of the 49ers during the Harbaugh years?**
    A. Patrick Willis
    B. NaVorro Bowman
    C. Aldon Smith
    D. All of the above

---

16. **Which 49ers running back was a key contributor during the Harbaugh years?**

A. Frank Gore
B. Carlos Hyde
C. Raheem Mostert
D. Matt Breida

---

17. **What was Jim Harbaugh's win-loss record during his tenure with the 49ers?**
    A. 44-19-1
    B. 38-22
    C. 49-16-1
    D. 36-24

---

18. **What was the 49ers' regular-season record in 2011, Jim Harbaugh's first year as head coach?**
    A. 10-6
    B. 12-4
    C. 13-3
    D. 9-7

---

19. **What stadium served as the 49ers' home during the Harbaugh years?**
    A. Levi's Stadium
    B. Candlestick Park
    C. Oracle Park
    D. Kezar Stadium

---

20. **What ultimately led to the end of Jim Harbaugh's tenure with the 49ers?**
    A. A losing season

B. Conflicts with team management
C. Player dissatisfaction
D. A lack of playoff success

Answers:

1. **Answer:** B. 2011
   Explanation: Jim Harbaugh became head coach in 2011 and immediately turned the franchise around.

2. **Answer:** B. New Orleans Saints
   Explainer: The 49ers beat Saints 36-32 in a thrilling NFC Divisional Round.

3. **Answer:** C. The Catch III
   Explanation: Vernon Davis's touchdown became known as "The Catch III," paying homage to earlier 49ers playoff moments.

4. **Answer:** A. Alex Smith
   Explanation: Alex Smith started the 2012 season but was replaced after an injury.

5. **Answer:** A. Alex Smith's injury
   Explanation: Smith suffered a concussion, leading to Colin Kaepernick becoming the starter.

6. **Answer:** A. Most rushing yards by a quarterback in a playoff game
   Explanation: Kaepernick rushed 181 yards against the Packers, setting an NFL playoff record.

7. **Answer:** B. Atlanta Falcons
   Explanation: The 49ers came back to defeat the Falcons in the NFC Championship Game, 28-24.

8. **Answer:** A. John Harbaugh
   Explanation: John Harbaugh, Jim's brother, coached the Ravens in Super Bowl XLVII.

9. **Answer:** A. 34-31
   Explanation: The Ravens defeated the 49ers in a dramatic Super Bowl XLVII.

10. **Answer:** C. The Harbaugh Bowl
    Explanation: Super Bowl XLVII was called "The Harbaugh Bowl."

11. **Answer:** D. Jacoby Jones
    Explanation: Jones returned a kickoff 108 yards for a Super Bowl touchdown.

12. **Answer:** A. A missed pass interference call
    Explanation: The 49ers argued a pass interference should have been called on the Ravens in the final moments.

13. **Answer:** C. Seattle Seahawks
    Explanation: The Seahawks eliminated the 49ers in the 2013 NFC Championship Game.

14. **Answer:** A. An interception that sealed the Seahawks' victory
    Explanation: Sherman's tipped pass led to an interception, ending the 49ers' Super Bowl hopes.

15. **Answer:** D. All of the above
    Explanation: Patrick Willis, NaVorro Bowman, and Aldon Smith were all key defensive players during this era.

16. **Answer:** A. Frank Gore
    Explanation: Gore was the team's workhorse running back throughout Harbaugh's tenure.

17. **Answer:** A. 44-19-1
    Explanation: Harbaugh had an impressive win-loss record, making him one of the most successful coaches in 49ers history.

18. **Answer:** C. 13-3
    Explanation: The 49ers finished 13-3 in Harbaugh's first season, a dramatic improvement.

19. **Answer:** B. Candlestick Park
    Explanation: The 49ers played at Candlestick Park until 2014.

---

20. **Answer:** B. Conflicts with team management
    Explanation: Harbaugh's tenure ended due to disagreements with the front office, despite his success.

Chapter 9

The Kyle Shanahan Era and Beyond (2017-Present)

Questions:

1. **Who became the head coach of the San Francisco 49ers in 2017?**
   A. Jim Harbaugh
   B. Kyle Shanahan
   C. Mike McDaniel
   D. Chip Kelly

2. **Who was hired as the general manager alongside Kyle Shanahan in 2017?**
   A. Trent Baalke
   B. John Lynch
   C. Jed York
   D. Mike McCarthy

3. **What was the 49ers' record during Kyle Shanahan's first season in 2017?**
   A. 4-12
   B. 6-10
   C. 8-8
   D. 5-11

4. **Which quarterback did the 49ers acquire via trade in 2017?**

A. Jimmy Garoppolo
B. Nick Mullens
C. Trey Lance
D. Blaine Gabbert

---

5. **What position does George Kittle play?**
   A. Wide Receiver
   B. Tight End
   C. Linebacker
   D. Offensive Tackle

---

6. **What year was Nick Bosa drafted by the 49ers?**
   A. 2018
   B. 2019
   C. 2020
   D. 2021

---

7. **What pick overall was Nick Bosa in the 2019 NFL Draft?**
   A. First
   B. Second
   C. Third
   D. Fourth

---

8. **What was the 49ers' regular season record in the 2019 season?**
   A. 10-6
   B. 12-4

C. 13-3
D. 14-2

---

9. **Which team did the 49ers defeat in the 2019 NFC Championship Game?**
   A. Green Bay Packers
   B. Seattle Seahawks
   C. New Orleans Saints
   D. Minnesota Vikings

---

10. **Which team did the 49ers face in Super Bowl LIV?**
    A. Kansas City Chiefs
    B. Baltimore Ravens
    C. New England Patriots
    D. Tampa Bay Buccaneers

---

11. **What was Super Bowl LIV's final score?**
    A. 31-20
    B. 34-31
    C. 28-24
    D. 27-20

---

12. **Who was named the 2019 NFL Defensive Rookie of the Year?**
    A. Fred Warner
    B. Nick Bosa
    C. Arik Armstead
    D. Solomon Thomas

13. **What was the 49ers' rushing yards total in the 2019 NFC Championship Game?**
    A. 220 yards
    B. 285 yards
    C. 300 yards
    D. 186 yards

14. **Which running back set a franchise playoff record with four rushing touchdowns in the 2019 NFC Championship Game?**
    A. Tevin Coleman
    B. Raheem Mostert
    C. Matt Breida
    D. Elijah Mitchell

15. **Who is the 49ers' defensive leader and play-caller under Kyle Shanahan?**
    A. Nick Bosa
    B. Fred Warner
    C. Dre Greenlaw
    D. Jaquiski Tartt

16. **What unique feature is part of Kyle Shanahan's offensive strategy?**
    A. Heavy use of play-action
    B. No-huddle offense
    C. Focus on deep passing
    D. Primarily running the ball

17. **Which 49ers player was named First-Team All-Pro multiple times under Shanahan's coaching?**
    A. George Kittle
    B. Nick Bosa
    C. Trent Williams
    D. All of the above

18. **What year did the 49ers return to the playoffs after their 2019 Super Bowl appearance?**
    A. 2020
    B. 2021
    C. 2022
    D. 2018

19. **Who replaced Jimmy Garoppolo as starting quarterback for the 2022 season?**
    A. Brock Purdy
    B. Trey Lance
    C. Nick Mullens
    C.J. Beathard

20. **What legacy has Kyle Shanahan built with the 49ers during his tenure?**
    A. Offensive innovation and defensive dominance
    B. Rebuilding without success
    C. Strong free agency focus
    D. Limited playoff appearances

Answers:

1. **Answer:** B. Kyle Shanahan
   Explanation: Shanahan became head coach in 2017, bringing his offensive expertise.

2. **Answer:** B. John Lynch
   Explanation: Lynch was hired as GM in 2017 and partnered with Shanahan to rebuild the team.

3. **Answer:** D. 6-10
   Explanation: The 49ers struggled in Shanahan's first season rebuilding the roster.

4. **Answer:** A. Jimmy Garoppolo
   Explanation: Garoppolo was acquired from the Patriots and became the starting quarterback.

5. **Answer:** B. Tight End
   Explanation: George Kittle is a dominant tight end known for his receiving and blocking skills.

6. **Answer:** B. 2019
   Explanation: Bosa was drafted in 2019 and made an immediate impact.

7. **Answer:** B. Second
   Explanation: Bosa was the second overall pick in the 2019 NFL Draft.

---

8. **Answer:** C. 13-3
   Explanation: The 49ers had a dominant regular season in 2019, finishing 13-3.

---

9. **Answer:** A. Green Bay Packers
   Explanation: The 49ers defeated the Packers 37-20 to advance to the Super Bowl.

---

10. **Answer:** A. Kansas City Chiefs
    Explanation: The 49ers faced Patrick Mahomes and the Chiefs in Super Bowl LIV.

---

11. **Answer:** A. 31-20
    Explanation: The Chiefs defeated the 49ers in a dramatic comeback victory.

---

12. **Answer:** B. Nick Bosa
    Explanation: Bosa was named Defensive Rookie of the Year for his outstanding performance.

---

13. **Answer:** B. 285 yards
    Explanation: The 49ers dominated the Packers with 285 yards.

---

14. **Answer:** B. Raheem Mostert
    Explainer: Mostert set franchise playoff record with four touchdowns.

---

15. **Answer:** B. Fred Warner
    Explanation: Warner is the defensive leader and signal-caller for the 49ers.

---

16. **Answer:** A. Heavy use of play-action
    Explanation: Shanahan's offense is known for its creative use of play-action.

---

17. **Answer:** D. All of the above
    Explanation: Kittle, Bosa, and Williams have all been named First-Team All-Pro under Shanahan.

---

18. **Answer:** B. 2021
    Explanation: The 49ers returned to the playoffs in 2021 after missing in 2020.

---

19. **Answer:** B. Trey Lance
    Explanation: Lance took over as the starting quarterback in the 2022 season before an injury.

---

20. **Answer:** A. Offensive innovation and defensive dominance
    Explanation: Shanahan's legacy includes creating a well-rounded, competitive team.

PART IV

THE LEGENDS AND THE RIVALRIES

Chapter 10

Players Who Defined the Franchise

Questions:

1. **Who is considered the greatest quarterback in San Francisco 49ers history?**
   A. Steve Young
   B. Colin Kaepernick
   C. Joe Montana
   D. John Brodie

2. **Which wide receiver holds the all-time record for receiving yards and touchdowns in NFL history?**
   A. Terrell Owens
   B. Jerry Rice
   C. Randy Moss
   D. Michael Crabtree

3. **What defensive position did Ronnie Lott primarily play for the 49ers?**
   A. Linebacker
   B. Cornerback
   C. Safety
   D. Defensive End

4. **Which player led the 49ers to four Super Bowl victories and was named Super Bowl MVP three times?**

A. Steve Young
B. Joe Montana
C. John Taylor
D. Frank Gore

---

5. **What running back is the all-time rushing leader for the 49ers?**
A. Frank Gore
B. Roger Craig
C. Ricky Watters
D. Garrison Hearst

---

6. **What position did Steve Young play for the 49ers?**
A. Running Back
B. Quarterback
C. Wide Receiver
D. Tight End

---

7. **Which player was known for his famous catch in the 1981 NFC Championship Game, dubbed "The Catch"?**
A. Jerry Rice
B. John Taylor
C. Dwight Clark
D. Brent Jones

---

8. **What was Joe Montana's nickname during his playing career?**
A. The Golden Boy

B. Joe Cool
C. The Comeback Kid
D. Big Game Joe

9. **Which 49ers player was named NFL MVP in 1992?**
A. Jerry Rice
B. Steve Young
C. Ronnie Lott
D. Joe Montana

10. **Which unsung hero caught the game-winning touchdown in Super Bowl XXIII?**
A. John Taylor
B. Roger Craig
C. Dwight Clark
D. Brent Jones

11. **What linebacker was known for his leadership on the 49ers' defense during the Harbaugh years?**
A. Patrick Willis
B. NaVorro Bowman
C. Fred Warner
D. Charles Haley

12. **What offensive lineman became a key protector for Joe Montana and Steve Young?**
A. Jesse Sapolu
B. Harris Barton

C. Joe Staley
D. Randy Cross

---

13. **Which fullback revolutionized the position with his versatility as a runner and receiver?**
A. Roger Craig
B. Frank Gore
C. Tom Rathman
D. Kyle Juszczyk

---

14. **What was Jerry Rice's signature nickname?**
A. Touchdown Machine
B. The Flash
C. The G.O.A.T.
D. World Class Rice

---

15. **Who is credited with creating the 49ers' dynasty by drafting key players like Joe Montana?**
A. Bill Walsh
B. George Seifert
C. Eddie DeBartolo Jr.
D. John McVay

---

16. **Which defender recorded a crucial interception in Super Bowl XIX?**
A. Ronnie Lott
B. Eric Wright
C. Fred Dean
D. Patrick Willis

17. **What tight end was a reliable target for Montana and Young during the 1980s and 1990s?**
A. Brent Jones
B. George Kittle
C. Dwight Clark
D. Vernon Davis

18. **Who was the 49ers' leading receiver in Super Bowl XXIII, catching 11 passes for 215 yards?**
A. John Taylor
B. Roger Craig
C. Jerry Rice
D. Brent Jones

19. **Which unsung hero made a pivotal fumble recovery in the 1994 NFC Championship Game?**
A. Merton Hanks
B. Tim McDonald
C. Eric Davis
D. Bryant Young

20. **What defensive end played a significant role in the 49ers' Super Bowl wins during the 1980s?**
A. Charles Haley
B. Fred Dean
C. Justin Smith
D. Aldon Smith

Answers:

1. **Answer:** C. Joe Montana
   Explanation: Montana is considered one of the greatest quarterbacks ever, leading the 49ers to four Super Bowl titles.

2. **Answer:** B. Jerry Rice
   Explanation: Rice is the NFL's all-time leader in receiving yards and touchdowns, solidifying his status as the greatest receiver.

3. **Answer:** C. Safety
   Explanation: Lott excelled at safety, known for his hard hits and leadership on defense.

4. **Answer:** B. Joe Montana
   Explanation: Montana won four Super Bowls with the 49ers and was named MVP in three.

5. **Answer:** A. Frank Gore
   Explanation: Gore is the 49ers' all-time leading rusher and one of the most consistent runners in NFL history.

6. **Answer:** B. Quarterback
   Explanation: Young was known for his dual-threat ability as a passer and runner.

7. **Answer:** C. Dwight Clark
   Explanation: Clark made "The Catch," one of the most iconic plays in NFL history, in the 1981 NFC Championship Game.

8. **Answer:** B. Joe Cool
   Explanation: Montana earned the nickname "Joe Cool" for his calm demeanor in high-pressure situations.

9. **Answer:** B. Steve Young
   Explanation: Young won the NFL MVP award in 1992, showcasing his dominance as a quarterback.

10. **Answer:** A. John Taylor
    Explanation: Taylor caught the game-winning touchdown in Super Bowl XXIII, a critical moment in 49ers history.

11. **Answer:** A. Patrick Willis
    Explanation: Willis was a dominant linebacker and the leader of the 49ers' defense during the Harbaugh era.

12. **Answer:** B. Harris Barton
    Explanation: Barton was a cornerstone of the 49ers' offensive line during their Super Bowl years.

13. **Answer:** A. Roger Craig

    Explanation: Craig was the first player in NFL history to record 1,000 rushing and 1,000 receiving yards in a single season.

14. **Answer:** C. The G.O.A.T.

    Explanation: Jerry Rice is widely known as "The G.O.A.T." (Greatest of All Time) for his accomplishments.

15. **Answer:** A. Bill Walsh

    Explanation: Walsh's strategic brilliance and draft picks built the 49ers' dynasty in the 1980s.

16. **Answer:** B. Eric Wright

    Explanation: Wright's interception in Super Bowl XIX helped the 49ers secure their victory.

17. **Answer:** A. Brent Jones

    Explanation: Jones was a reliable tight end and a key part of the 49ers' passing attack.

18. **Answer:** C. Jerry Rice

    Explanation: Rice had a legendary performance in Super Bowl XXIII, earning MVP honors.

19. **Answer:** C. Eric Davis
    Explanation: Davis made a pivotal fumble recovery in the 1994 NFC Championship Game against the Cowboys.

20. **Answer:** A. Charles Haley
    Explanation: Haley was a dominant defensive end contributing multiple Super Bowl wins for the 49ers.

Chapter 11

Coaches and Innovators

Questions:

1. **Who is credited with creating the West Coast Offense?**
   A. Mike Shanahan
   B. Bill Walsh
   C. Jim Harbaugh
   D. Kyle Shanahan

---

2. **What year did Bill Walsh become the head coach of the San Francisco 49ers?**
   A. 1979
   B. 1981
   C. 1983
   D. 1985

---

3. **What was Bill Walsh's first major accomplishment as head coach?**
   A. Winning the NFC West
   B. Winning the Super Bowl in 1981
   C. Developing the West Coast Offense
   D. Drafting Joe Montana

---

4. **Which coach succeeded Bill Walsh and led the 49ers to two Super Bowl victories?**
   A. George Seifert

B. Mike Shanahan
C. Jim Harbaugh
D. Kyle Shanahan

---

5. **Who was the offensive coordinator for the 49ers during their Super Bowl wins in the late 1980s?**
A. Mike Holmgren
B. Mike Shanahan
C. Norv Turner
D. Gary Kubiak

---

6. **What innovative strategy is Bill Walsh best known for?**
A. No-huddle offense
B. Heavy use of play-action passing
C. Short, precise passing as an extension of the run game
D. Vertical passing game

---

7. **Which head coach led the 49ers to the Super Bowl in 2012?**
A. Mike Nolan
B. Jim Harbaugh
C. Mike Singletary
D. Kyle Shanahan

---

8. **What was Jim Harbaugh's signature motivational slogan?**
A. "Win at all costs."
B. "We want winners."

C. "Who's got it better than us?"
D. "Do your job."

9. **What was Kyle Shanahan's first season as 49ers head coach?**
   A. 2016
   B. 2017
   C. 2018
   D. 2019

10. **Which team did the 49ers face in the Super Bowl during Kyle Shanahan's tenure?**
    A. Baltimore Ravens
    B. Kansas City Chiefs
    C. Seattle Seahawks
    D. New England Patriots

11. **What role did Mike Shanahan have with the 49ers during the 1990s?**
    A. Head Coach
    B. Defensive Coordinator
    C. Offensive Coordinator
    D. Quarterbacks Coach

12. **What unique aspect of Kyle Shanahan's offense has drawn praise across the NFL?**
    A. Run-heavy schemes with creative motion
    B. Deep passing emphasis

C. Relying on screen passes

D. Frequent trick plays

---

13. **Who was the head coach during the 49ers' 1994 Super Bowl-winning season?**

A. Bill Walsh

B. George Seifert

C. Mike Shanahan

D. Steve Mariucci

---

14. **What was Bill Walsh's nickname due to his strategic brilliance?**

A. The Professor

B. The Genius

C. The Mastermind

D. The Strategist

---

15. **What was a defining feature of Jim Harbaugh's coaching style?**

A. Aggressive defensive schemes

B. Emotional intensity and physical toughness

C. Pass-heavy offensive focus

D. Special teams innovation

---

16. **Which coach led the 49ers to three consecutive NFC Championship Games from 2011 to 2013?**

A. Kyle Shanahan

B. Jim Harbaugh

C. Mike Nolan

D. George Seifert

---

17. **What year did George Seifert replace Bill Walsh as head coach?**
    A. 1987
    B. 1988
    C. 1989
    D. 1990

---

18. **Who was the first 49ers head coach to win five Super Bowl titles?**
    A. Bill Walsh
    B. George Seifert
    C. No coach won five titles
    D. Kyle Shanahan

---

19. **What was a key reason for Kyle Shanahan's success with the 49ers?**
    A. Drafting elite quarterbacks
    B. Building a balanced team with a dominant defense and creative offense
    C. Developing strong special teams
    D. Trading for veteran superstars

---

20. **What is the legacy of Bill Walsh's West Coast Offense?**
    A. Revolutionizing modern football with a focus on quick, precise passing

B. Setting NFL records for rushing yards
C. Creating the no-huddle offense
D. Specializing in defensive schemes

Answers:

1. **Answer:** B. Bill Walsh
   Explanation: Walsh created the West Coast Offense, revolutionizing NFL strategy.

---

2. **Answer:** A. 1979
   Explanation: Walsh became head coach in 1979 and quickly turned the franchise around.

---

3. **Answer:** B. Winning the Super Bowl in 1981
   Explanation: Walsh led the 49ers to their first Super Bowl title, establishing their dominance.

---

4. **Answer:** A. George Seifert
   Explanation: Seifert succeeded Walsh and maintained the 49ers' championship legacy.

---

5. **Answer:** B. Mike Shanahan
   Explanation: Shanahan was the offensive coordinator during the 1994 Super Bowl-winning season.

---

6. **Answer:** C. Short, precise passing as an extension of the run game
   Explanation: This hallmark of the West Coast Offense became a staple in modern football.

7. **Answer:** B. Jim Harbaugh
   Explainer: Harbaugh led the 49ers in Super Bowl
   XLVII against the Baltimore Ravens.

---

8. **Answer:** C. "Who's got it better than us?"
   Explanation: Harbaugh's slogan inspired his players
   and became iconic during his tenure.

---

9. **Answer:** B. 2017
   Explanation: Shanahan took over as head coach in 2017
   and began rebuilding the team.

---

10. **Answer:** B. Kansas City Chiefs
    Explanation: The 49ers faced the Chiefs in Super Bowl
    LIV, losing 31-20.

---

11. **Answer:** C. Offensive Coordinator
    Explanation: Mike Shanahan played a key role as the
    offensive coordinator during the 49ers' 1990s success.

---

12. **Answer:** A. Run-heavy schemes with creative motion
    Explanation: Shanahan's offensive system emphasizes
    creative motion and efficient running plays.

---

13. **Answer:** B. George Seifert
    Explanation: Seifert coached the 49ers to their 1994 Super Bowl victory.

14. **Answer:** B. The Genius
    Explanation: Walsh earned the nickname "The Genius" for his innovative strategies.

15. **Answer:** B. Emotional intensity and physical toughness
    Explanation: Harbaugh emphasized physicality and emotional leadership.

16. **Answer:** B. Jim Harbaugh
    Explainer: Harbaugh led the 49ers to three NFC Championship Games.

17. **Answer:** C. 1989
    Explanation: Seifert replaced Walsh in 1989 and won the Super Bowl in his first season.

18. **Answer:** C. No coach won five titles
    Explanation: No single coach won all five 49ers Super Bowl championships; they were split between Walsh and Seifert.

19. **Answer:** B. Building a balanced team with a dominant defense and creative offense
    Explanation: Shanahan's success came from his ability to create well-rounded teams.

---

20. **Answer:** A. Revolutionizing modern football with a focus on quick, precise passing
    Explanation: Walsh's West Coast Offense changed the way football is played, influencing countless coaches and teams.

Chapter 12

Rivalries That Made History

Questions:

1. **Which team has been considered the 49ers' most iconic rival since the 1970s?**
   A. Dallas Cowboys
   B. Green Bay Packers
   C. Seattle Seahawks
   D. Los Angeles Rams

2. **What famous play occurred during the 1981 NFC Championship Game against the Dallas Cowboys?**
   A. The Drive
   B. The Catch
   C. The Tackle
   D. The Miracle Pass

3. **Who caught "The Catch" in the 1981 NFC Championship Game?**
   A. Jerry Rice
   B. Dwight Clark
   C. John Taylor
   D. Brent Jones

4. **What was the result of the 1994 NFC Championship Game between the 49ers and the Cowboys?**
   A. Cowboys victory, 28-17

B. 49ers victory, 38-28
C. 49ers victory, 30-20
D. Cowboys victory, 31-27

---

5. **Which quarterback led the 49ers to victory in the 1994 NFC Championship Game?**
   A. Joe Montana
   B. Steve Young
   C. Jeff Garcia
   D. Alex Smith

---

6. **What was the significance of the 1998 NFC Wild Card Game against the Green Bay Packers?**
   A. The game was decided by "The Catch II"
   B. It was Brett Favre's first playoff loss
   C. The Packers shut out the 49ers
   D. It ended with a missed field goal

---

7. **Who caught "The Catch II" in the 1998 NFC Wild Card Game?**
   A. Jerry Rice
   B. Terrell Owens
   C. John Taylor
   D. George Kittle

---

8. **Which team eliminated the 49ers from the playoffs in three consecutive seasons (1995-1997)?**
   A. Dallas Cowboys
   B. Seattle Seahawks

C. Green Bay Packers
D. New York Giants

---

9. **What year did the rivalry with the Seattle Seahawks intensify with the arrival of Pete Carroll?**
   A. 2009
   B. 2010
   C. 2011
   D. 2012

---

10. **Which famous play defined the 2013 NFC Championship Game between the 49ers and the Seahawks?**
    A. Richard Sherman's tip
    B. Colin Kaepernick's scramble
    C. Frank Gore's touchdown run
    D. A blocked field goal

---

11. **Who was the Seahawks quarterback during their 2013 rivalry game with the 49ers?**
    A. Matt Hasselbeck
    B. Russell Wilson
    C. Geno Smith
    D. Tarvaris Jackson

---

12. **Which team ended the 49ers' undefeated season in 2019?**
    A. Dallas Cowboys
    B. Green Bay Packers

C. Seattle Seahawks

D. Baltimore Ravens

---

13. **What was the result of the 2019 NFC Championship Game against the Green Bay Packers?**
    A. Packers victory, 31-28
    B. 49ers victory, 37-20
    C. Packers victory, 24-20
    D. 49ers victory, 30-17

---

14. **What was the 49ers' record against the Cowboys in playoff matchups during the 1990s?**
    A. 1-2
    B. 2-1
    C. 0-3
    D. 3-0

---

15. **Which rivalry is known as the "Battle of the West"?**
    A. 49ers vs. Seahawks
    B. 49ers vs. Rams
    C. 49ers vs. Packers
    D. 49ers vs. Cowboys

---

16. **What player famously intercepted a Tony Romo pass to secure a 49ers win in 2014?**
    A. NaVorro Bowman
    B. Eric Reid
    C. Patrick Willis
    D. Aldon Smith

17. **Who was the 49ers' head coach during the peak of their rivalry with the Green Bay Packers in the 1990s?**
A. George Seifert
B. Mike Shanahan
C. Steve Mariucci
D. Bill Walsh

18. **What controversial moment occurred during the 1998 Wild Card Game against the Packers?**
A. A fumble that wasn't called
B. A missed pass interference call
C. Jerry Rice's non-fumble being ruled incomplete
D. Terrell Owens dropping a game-winning pass

19. **Which rivalry game was dubbed "The Statement Game" in the 2019 season?**
A. 49ers vs. Seahawks
B. 49ers vs. Packers
C. 49ers vs. Ravens
D. 49ers vs. Saints

20. **What legacy did the 49ers' rivalries leave on the NFL?**
A. Elevated playoff drama and iconic moments
B. The creation of the West Coast Offense
C. Innovations in defensive schemes
D. Player-coach rivalries

Answers:

1. **Answer:** A. Dallas Cowboys
   Explanation: The rivalry with the Cowboys, particularly in the 1970s and 1990s, defined an era of NFC dominance.

2. **Answer:** B. The Catch
   Explanation: Dwight Clark's leaping grab in the 1981 NFC Championship Game is one of the most iconic moments in NFL history.

3. **Answer:** B. Dwight Clark
   Explanation: Clark made "The Catch" from a pass by Joe Montana, securing the 49ers' win over the Cowboys.

4. **Answer:** B. 49ers victory, 38-28
   Explanation: The 49ers defeated the Cowboys in the 1994 NFC Championship Game en route to their fifth Super Bowl win.

5. **Answer:** B. Steve Young
   Explanation: Young led the 49ers to victory in the 1994 NFC Championship Game.

6. **Answer:** A. The game was decided by "The Catch II"
   Explanation: Terrell Owens caught a dramatic touchdown to win the 1998 NFC Wild Card Game.

---

7. **Answer:** B. Terrell Owens
   Explanation: Owens made "The Catch II," solidifying his place in 49ers history.

---

8. **Answer:** C. Green Bay Packers
   Explanation: The Packers eliminated the 49ers from the playoffs three consecutive times in the late 1990s.

---

9. **Answer:** B. 2010
   Explanation: Pete Carroll's arrival in Seattle heightened the rivalry with the 49ers.

---

10. **Answer:** A. Richard Sherman's tip
    Explanation: Sherman tipped a Kaepernick pass to secure the Seahawks' victory in the 2013 NFC Championship Game.

---

11. **Answer:** B. Russell Wilson
    Explanation: Wilson was the Seahawks' quarterback and played a key role in their rivalry with the 49ers.

---

12. **Answer:** C. Seattle Seahawks
    Explanation: The Seahawks defeated the 49ers in overtime to hand them their first loss of the 2019 season.

---

13. **Answer:** B. 49ers victory, 37-20
    Explanation: The 49ers dominated the Packers in the 2019 NFC Championship Game to advance to Super Bowl LIV.

---

14. **Answer:** A. 1-2
    Explanation: The Cowboys defeated the 49ers in two playoff matchups during the 1990s, with the 49ers winning one.

---

15. **Answer:** A. 49ers vs. Seahawks
    Explanation: This NFC West rivalry is called the "Battle of the West."

---

16. **Answer:** B. Eric Reid
    Explanation: Reid's Romo interception was a crucial play in securing a 49ers victory.

---

17. **Answer:** C. Steve Mariucci
    Explanation: Mariucci coached the 49ers during their heated rivalry with the Packers in the 1990s.

---

18. **Answer:** C. Jerry Rice's non-fumble being ruled incomplete
   Explanation: A controversial call allowed the 49ers to maintain possession and win the game.

19. **Answer:** D. 49ers vs. Saints
   Explanation: The 49ers defeated the Saints in a high-scoring thriller, proving their dominance in the 2019 season.

20. **Answer:** A. Elevated playoff drama and iconic moments
   Explanation: The 49ers' rivalries have left a lasting impact on the NFL with unforgettable games and dramatic finishes.

PART V

FAN CULTURE AND MEMORABLE MOMENTS

Chapter 13

The Faithful 49ers Fans

Questions:

1. **What nickname is used to describe the loyal fanbase of the San Francisco 49ers?**
   A. The Gold Rush
   B. The Red Sea
   C. The Faithful
   D. The Niner Gang

2. **What year did the 49ers play their final game at Candlestick Park?**
   A. 2012
   B. 2013
   C. 2014
   D. 2015

3. **Which famous 49ers tradition involved fans waving red flags at Candlestick Park?**
   A. The Wave
   B. Faithful Flags
   C. Red Flag Rally
   D. Niners' Pride

4. **What is the name of the 49ers' current home stadium?**
   A. Levi's Stadium
   B. Oracle Park

C. Kezar Stadium
D. Candlestick Arena

---

5. **What city is Levi's Stadium?**
   A. San Francisco
   B. Oakland
   C. Santa Clara
   D. San Jose

---

6. **Which 49ers tradition involves tailgating before games?**
   A. Parking Lot Party
   B. Faithful Feast
   C. Niner Tailgate
   D. Gold Lot Gatherings

---

7. **What chant do 49ers fans commonly shout during games?**
   A. "Go Niners!"
   B. "Who's Got It Better Than Us?"
   C. "Faithful, Rise Up!"
   D. "We Are The Faithful!"

---

8. **What year did the 49ers officially move to Levi's Stadium?**
   A. 2012
   B. 2013
   C. 2014
   D. 2015

9. **What was Candlestick Park's nickname due to its windy conditions?**
    A. The Breezy Dome
    B. The Stick
    C. The Whirlwind Stadium
    D. The Candlestick Gale

10. **What is the largest group of 49ers fans outside the United States?**
    A. Gold Rush Australia
    B. Niners United UK
    C. Faithful Mexico
    D. Red and Gold Germany

11. **What iconic moment is known as "The Last Hurrah" at Candlestick Park?**
    A. Steve Young's final game
    B. Joe Montana's return
    C. NaVorro Bowman's pick-six against the Falcons
    D. Jerry Rice's retirement ceremony

12. **What is the fan zone area at Levi's Stadium called?**
    A. Gold Zone
    B. Faithful Lounge
    C. Red Zone Rally
    D. Niners Nation

13. **What special feature at Levi's Stadium allows fans to view historical memorabilia?**
    A. Hall of Champions
    B. 49ers Museum
    C. Faithful Vault
    D. Gold Rush Exhibit

14. **What group performs during games to energize the crowd?**
    A. Niners Spirit Squad
    B. Gold Rush Cheerleaders
    C. Faithful Dancers
    D. Red & Gold Crew

15. **What is the 49ers' official anthem, often played during home games?**
    A. "We Are The Champions"
    B. "Bang Bang Niner Gang"
    C. "Faithful Forever"
    D. "Glory Days"

16. **Which feature of Levi's Stadium is designed to honor the team's history?**
    A. The Legacy Wall
    B. The Ring of Honor
    C. The Hall of Fame Concourse
    D. The Golden Era Exhibit

17. **What pre-game activity is a staple for 49ers fans?**
    A. Marching Parade
    B. Niners Tailgate Cookout
    C. Gold Rush Walk
    D. The Red Run Rally

18. **How do 49ers fans collectively relate?**
    A. Niners Forever
    B. The Faithful
    C. The Gold Gang
    D. Red and Gold Warriors

19. **Which player's jersey is among the most commonly worn by 49ers fans at games?**
    A. Joe Montana
    B. Jerry Rice
    C. Steve Young
    D. All of the above

20. **What is the legacy of "The Faithful" in 49ers history?**
    A. Supporting the team through ups and downs
    B. Creating a family atmosphere in the stands
    C. Building traditions that span decades
    D. All of the above

Answers:

1. **Answer:** C. The Faithful
   Explanation: The 49ers fanbase is known as "The Faithful" for their unwavering support.

2. **Answer:** B. 2013
   Explainer: The 49ers played Candlestick Park December 2013.

3. **Answer:** B. Faithful Flags
   Explanation: Fans waving red flags at Candlestick became a signature tradition.

4. **Answer:** A. Levi's Stadium
   Explanation: The 49ers moved to Levi's Stadium in 2014.

5. **Answer:** C. Santa Clara
   Explanation: Levi's Stadium is in Santa Clara, not San Francisco.

6. **Answer:** D. Gold Lot Gatherings
   Explanation: Tailgating is a cherished tradition for 49ers fans in designated Gold Lot areas.

7. **Answer:** B. "Who's Got It Better Than Us?"
   Explanation: This chant became popular during Jim Harbaugh's tenure as head coach.

---

8. **Answer:** C. 2014
   Explanation: The 49ers began playing at Levi's Stadium in the 2014 season.

---

9. **Answer:** B. The Stick
   Explanation: Candlestick Park earned the nickname "The Stick" due to its unique conditions.

---

10. **Answer:** D. Red and Gold Germany
    Explanation: Germany hosts one of the largest groups of international 49ers fans.

---

11. **Answer:** C. NaVorro Bowman's pick-six against the Falcons
    Explanation: Bowman's iconic play sealed the 49ers' final victory at Candlestick.

---

12. **Answer:** A. Gold Zone
    Explanation: The fan zone area at Levi's Stadium is known as the Gold Zone.

---

13. **Answer:** B. 49ers Museum
Explanation: Levi's Stadium houses the 49ers Museum, showcasing the team's history.

---

14. **Answer:** B. Gold Rush Cheerleaders
Explanation: The Gold Rush Cheerleaders perform at home games to energize the crowd.

---

15. **Answer:** B. "Bang Bang Niner Gang"
Explanation: This song has become an anthem for 49ers fans during games.

---

16. **Answer:** B. The Ring of Honor
Explanation: The Ring of Honor at Levi's Stadium celebrates the team's legendary players.

---

17. **Answer:** B. Niners Tailgate Cookout
Explanation: Tailgating is a pre-game ritual for many 49ers fans.

---

18. **Answer:** B. The Faithful
Explanation: Fans proudly call themselves "The Faithful" to reflect their loyalty.

---

19. **Answer:** D. All of the above
    Explanation: Montana, Rice, and Young jerseys are among the most popular at games.

---

20. **Answer:** D. All of the above
    Explanation: "The Faithful" have built a legacy of loyalty, traditions, and a family-like atmosphere.

Chapter 14

Iconic Plays and Games

Questions:

1. **What play is known as "The Catch," which helped the 49ers defeat the Dallas Cowboys in the 1981 NFC Championship Game?**
   A. Joe's Miracle Pass
   B. The Drive
   C. The Catch
   D. The Post

2. **Who threw the pass that resulted in "The Catch"?**
   A. Steve Young
   B. Joe Montana
   C. Jeff Garcia
   D. Alex Smith

3. **Which player made "The Catch II" in the 1998 NFC Wild Card Game against the Green Bay Packers?**
   A. Jerry Rice
   B. Terrell Owens
   C. Dwight Clark
   D. Brent Jones

4. **What was the final score of Super Bowl XXIII, where the 49ers defeated the Cincinnati Bengals with a game-winning drive?**

A. 20-16
B. 24-21
C. 27-24
D. 31-28

5. **Who caught the game-winning touchdown pass in Super Bowl XXIII?**
A. Jerry Rice
B. Roger Craig
C. John Taylor
D. Brent Jones

6. **What 49ers running back set a playoff record with four rushing touchdowns in the 2019 NFC Championship Game?**
A. Tevin Coleman
B. Frank Gore
C. Raheem Mostert
D. Ricky Watters

7. **Which defensive game is known as "The Pick at the Stick"?**
A. Patrick Willis intercepting Russell Wilson
B. Eric Reid's game-sealing interception
C. NaVorro Bowman's pick-six against the Falcons
D. Ronnie Lott's interception in Super Bowl XVI

8. **Which iconic 49ers play was a result of Richard Sherman tipping a pass in the 2013 NFC**

Championship Game?
A. "The Sherman Tip"
B. "The Deflection"
C. "The Interception"
D. "The Shutout Play"

9. **What play in Super Bowl XIX symbolized Joe Montana's dominance over Dan Marino and the Miami Dolphins?**
A. The Catch III
B. Montana's 44-yard touchdown pass to Jerry Rice
C. Montana's rushing touchdown
D. Montana's perfect QB sneak

10. **What game did Jerry Rice catch a career-long 96-yard touchdown pass?**
A. 1987 NFC Championship Game
B. 1988 regular season game against the Rams
C. 1994 Super Bowl
D. 1989 divisional round

11. **What was the pivotal play in the 2019 regular season that secured the 49ers' NFC West title?**
A. A blocked punt
B. Jimmy Garoppolo's game-winning touchdown pass
C. Dre Greenlaw's goal-line tackle against the Seahawks
D. Nick Bosa's strip-sack

12. **Who scored the first touchdown for the 49ers in Super Bowl XXIV, their 55-10 victory over the Denver Broncos?**
    A. Jerry Rice
    B. John Taylor
    C. Roger Craig
    D. Brent Jones

---

13. **Which 49ers game is known as "The Mud Bowl"?**
    A. 1984 NFC Championship Game against the Bears
    B. 1992 divisional round against the Redskins
    C. 1970 playoff game against the Cowboys
    D. 1994 NFC Championship Game

---

14. **Which 49ers quarterback orchestrated "The Drive" against the Cincinnati Bengals in Super Bowl XXIII?**
    A. Steve Young
    B. Joe Montana
    C. Colin Kaepernick
    D. Alex Smith

---

15. **What play in the 1994 NFC Championship Game against the Cowboys helped secure a 49ers victory?**
    A. Deion Sanders' pick-six
    B. Eric Davis' interception return for a touchdown
    C. Jerry Rice's 80-yard touchdown catch
    D. Brent Jones' red-zone reception

---

16. What was the name of the 1989 regular-season game in which Joe Montana led the 49ers to a 92-yard game-winning drive in the final moments?
A. "The Comeback"
B. "The Perfect Drive"
C. "The Last Minute"
D. "The Miracle on Grass"

17. Which defensive player made a critical fumble recovery in the 1984 NFC Championship Game?
A. Fred Dean
B. Ronnie Lott
C. Eric Wright
D. NaVorro Bowman

18. What iconic play marked Colin Kaepernick's 181-yard rushing performance in the 2012 NFC Divisional Round?
A. "The Long Run"
B. "The Read Option Dash"
C. "The Kaepernick Streak"
D. "The Run Game Revolution"

19. What memorable play occurred in the 1981 NFC Divisional Round against the New York Giants?
A. Ronnie Lott's game-sealing interception
B. Joe Montana's first playoff touchdown pass
C. Dwight Clark's two-touchdown performance
D. Fred Dean's critical sack

20. **What legacy do iconic 49ers games have in NFL history?**
    A. Setting standards for clutch performances
    B. Revolutionizing offensive and defensive playbooks
    C. Creating memorable playoff moments
    D. All of the above

Answers:

1. **Answer:** C. The Catch
   Explanation: Dwight Clark's leaping catch secured the 49ers' victory over the Cowboys in the 1981 NFC Championship Game.

2. **Answer:** B. Joe Montana
   Explanation: Montana threw the famous pass that led to "The Catch."

3. **Answer:** B. Terrell Owens
   Explanation: Owens made "The Catch II" in the 1998 NFC Wild Card Game against the Packers.

4. **Answer:** A. 20-16
   Explanation: The 49ers defeated the Bengals 20-16 in Super Bowl XXIII with a dramatic late-game drive.

5. **Answer:** C. John Taylor
   Explanation: Taylor caught the game-winning touchdown in Super Bowl XXIII.

6. **Answer:** C. Raheem Mostert
   Explanation: Mostert's four rushing touchdowns in the 2019 NFC Championship Game set a record.

7. **Answer:** C. NaVorro Bowman's pick-six against the Falcons
Explanation: Bowman's pick-six sealed the 49ers' final game at Candlestick Park.

---

8. **Answer:** A. "The Sherman Tip"
Explanation: Richard Sherman's tipped pass led to an interception, sending the Seahawks to the Super Bowl.

---

9. **Answer:** C. Montana's rushing touchdown
Explanation: Montana's versatility was on display in Super Bowl XIX with a rushing touchdown.

---

10. **Answer:** B. 1988 regular season game against the Rams
Explanation: Rice's career-long 96-yard touchdown catch came during a regular-season game.

---

11. **Answer:** C. Dre Greenlaw's goal-line tackle against the Seahawks
Explanation: Greenlaw's tackle secured the NFC West title for the 49ers in 2019.

---

12. **Answer:** A. Jerry Rice
Explanation: Rice scored the first touchdown in the 49ers' dominant Super Bowl XXIV win.

---

13. **Answer:** A. 1984 NFC Championship Game against the Bears
Explanation: The "Mud Bowl" was played in challenging conditions, with the 49ers emerging victorious.

14. **Answer:** B. Joe Montana
Explanation: Montana's calm demeanor led the 49ers on a 92-yard drive to win Super Bowl XXIII.

15. **Answer:** B. Eric Davis' interception return for a touchdown
Explanation: Davis' early pick-six set the tone for the 49ers' win over the Cowboys.

16. **Answer:** C. "The Last Minute"
Explanation: Montana led a legendary game-winning drive in the final moments of this 1989 game.

17. **Answer:** B. Ronnie Lott
Explanation: Lott's fumble recovery in the 1984 NFC Championship Game was pivotal.

18. **Answer:** B. "The Read Option Dash"
Explanation: Kaepernick's rushing dominance redefined the quarterback position in the playoffs.

19. **Answer:** A. Ronnie Lott's game-sealing interception
    Explanation: Lott's interception against the Giants highlighted his defensive prowess.

---

20. **Answer:** D. All of the above
    Explanation: The 49ers' iconic plays are integral to the NFL's rich history of thrilling moments.

Printed in Dunstable, United Kingdom